365 WAYS TO
SIMPLIFY
YOUR WORK LIFE

IDEAS THAT BRING MORE TIME, FREEDOM
AND SATISFACTION TO DAILY WORK

★

O D E T T E　　P O L L A R

Published by Dearborn Financial Publishing, Inc.®

Printed in the United States of America

96 97 98 10 9 8 7 6 5 4 3 2 1

Library of Congress Cataloging-in-Publication Data

Pollar, Odette
    365 ways to simplify your work life / Odette Pollar.
       p.   cm.
    Includes index.
    ISBN 0-7931-2281-3 (pbk.)
1. Time management. 2. Life skills. I. Title.
HD69. T54P65 1996   96-22812
650.1—dc20   CIP

More Advance Praise

"You should read *365 Ways to Simplify Your Work Life* every day. There are pearls of wisdom in it that will make a big difference in your life."

—Ken Blanchard, Coauthor
The One Minute Manager

"*365 Ways* is appealingly practical, commonsense, no-nonsense advice in small bites. Even for those who are reasonably organized already, it's icing on the cake, a chance to hone your art."

—Shelly Ginenthal, Director of Human Resources
Macworld Communications Inc.

"You don't just 'happen' to simplify life; you make a conscious decision and take action. This book outlines the process."

—Dianna Booher, Author
Get a Life and *Communicate with Confidence*

"Get your highlighter out and dive into this gold mine of brilliant ideas for simplifying your work life. You'll be glad you did, and so will the other important people in your life."

—George Morrisey, CSP, CPAE, Author
Creating Your Future: Personal Strategic Planning for Professionals

"*365 Ways to Simplify Your Work Life* has 365 immediately usable ideas!"

—Judith E. Sirkis, Partner
Lewis & Roca LLP, Lawyers

"With this book, author Odette Pollar gives us all a very precious gift, a gift frequently difficult to find these days—the gift of time. Don't waste another minute. Read this book now."

—Allen Klein, Author
The Healing Power of Humor, Quotations to Cheer You Up and *Wing Tips*

"Once again Odette makes so simple what all of us take for granted . . . that time is our single greatest asset."

—John Ermatinger, Vice President
Levi Strauss North America, Operations and Sourcing

"*365 Ways to Simplify Your Work Life* is loaded with fast, easy-to-read, clear concepts that can be implemented immediately. Great book!"

—Daniel Burris, Technology Forecaster and Futurist, Author
Technotrends

To Richard for all his patience
For my parents, who are always magnificent

CONTENTS

IN THE DAY-TO-DAY RUSH, it sometimes seems like we just don't have the time to sit down and get organized. The information superhighway, two-career families, child-care *dis*organization and downsizing—never before have there been so many competing claims on our time!

Many people are surprised to learn that getting and staying organized doesn't require a tremendous time commitment. It takes just a few minutes here to keep your desk organized, a few minutes there to make tasks more efficient, a few easy strategies to get more done in less time—and the payoff in improved productivity, efficiency and peace of mind is incalculable.

As the "founder" of the field of professional organizing, I welcome Odette Pollar's book *365 Ways to Simplify Your Work Life*, which is designed with exactly this busy reader in mind. It is filled with lots of clever and useful "quick-action" ideas to help make you more productive by simplifying how you work.

As you go through the day, pick and choose those ideas that will uncomplicate and ease your life. Be happily surprised at how slipping in a few "productivity" techniques each day can really lead you along the road to organization.

Enjoy the book, I certainly did!

—*Stephanie Winston*

WOULD YOU LIKE TO HAVE more time? Have a sense of satisfaction at the end of each day? Be able to go home feeling free from the pressures of the workplace? Help is on the way!

In our speeded-up lives, many of us go to workplaces rife with dissatisfactions, unrealistic expectations and frenetic changes. It's no wonder a majority of working people—at least some of the time—feel tired, irritated, unsatisfied or unhappy. Even in the best work situations, the pace of change and the exponential growth of information can be the cause of stress, burnout or a sense that there's no relief in sight. Until now.

If you want to focus on ways to ease your stress, reduce your load and simplify the complexities in the daily work you do, *365 Ways to Simplify Your Work Life* is for you. The book features hundreds of ideas to save time and improve results. You'll learn ways to bring more balance, satisfaction and fun back into your work. How? As you begin to use these tips, you'll be able to:

- Identify actions you can take right now to get out of the suffocating maze of demands, obligations and never-ending details.

- Add more freedom and satisfaction to your work life by taking small steps every day.

- Make technology and all those so-called labor-saving devices work *for* you instead of enslave you.

- Streamline your work flow using simple, proven organizing tools and tactics.

Using these 365 proven tips, suggestions and practical ideas, you, too, can step back and find ways to simplify your work life. I know it can be done, because for the past 15 years, I've helped thousands of people do just that.

Working as a management consultant, speaker, trainer and coach in the field of personal productivity, I have instructed both executives and workers in companies large and small, profit and nonprofit, all across the country on more effective ways to structure their time and businesses. I have worked with private clients to help bring balance back into their lives. These practical, often basic strategies have worked for people in all kinds of working situations. And they'll work for you.

How to Use This Book

Make this book your own. Read through it, mark it up and add your own ideas. Use it as a springboard to simplify team activities. You can try the ideas on for size to see if they'll work for you. Introduce one new thing each day or initiate several changes at once. If you have specific problem areas—whether the computer, your desk, phone or business travel—you will find plenty of ideas sprinkled throughout the text. If you want to review all the items related to a particular category, you can find them all by checking out the index.

There's also a chance for you to contribute your own ideas. At the end of the book, you'll find forms that you can fill out to share your insights about the book or add your own ideas for future editions. I would love to hear from you.

Happy simplifying!

THESE OBSERVATIONS came from many sources. All are a result of someone's hard work and repeated attempts to keep it simple!

My sincere thanks to Helen Argyres, Steve Benson, Larry Mann, Peggy Darland, my parents, Lynn Ballou and Linda Bine for ideas and suggestions; Wally Bock for his computer expertise; Nancy Pino for manuscript preparation; Ann Goodwin for editing; and Richard Witt for ideas, support and patience, always patience.

365 WAYS TO SIMPLIFY YOUR WORK LIFE

★ ★ ★ 1 ★ ★ ★

When traveling to a different time zone, leave
your digital watch at home—you know, the one
with built-in functions that requires complicated
instructions to adjust the time setting.
Carry an inexpensive analog watch that resets
the old-fashioned way.

★ ★ ★ 2 ★ ★ ★

Avoid faxing more than ten pages.
It is costly and ties up the equipment for others.

★ ★ ★ 3 ★ ★ ★

Simplify in every way. Eliminate the
unimportant, whether it be relationships, tasks,
responsibilities, possessions or beliefs.
Organize the remainder.

3

★ ★ ★ 4 ★ ★ ★

Streamline but do not sterilize. Some of those
UFOs—unidentified funny objects—should
remain in your life. They make you smile.

★ ★ ★ 5 ★ ★ ★

Use a tickler file with a folder for each
month and a folder for every day. Put birthday
cards for colleagues, invoices, airline tickets
and follow-up calls in the appropriate day
and month.

★ ★ ★ 6 ★ ★ ★

When possible, group meetings together—
either all in the morning or all in the afternoon.

4

★ ★ ★ 7 ★ ★ ★

If your administrative systems are a mess,
a computer will quickly double that mess.
Computers can produce paper faster than
you can dispose of it.

★ ★ ★ 8 ★ ★ ★

Store little-used items farther away. Even on a
shelf, keep the less-used items in the back and
keep those items you use frequently in the
front of the storage space.

5

★ ★ ★ 9 ★ ★ ★

6

Take a refresher course on time
management each year.

★ ★ ★ 10 ★ ★ ★

When information is not critical, instead
of interrupting your assistant or colleague, send
the information via phone mail or electronic
mail, even if he or she is next door.

★ ★ ★ 11 ★ ★ ★

Accept that others know more than you
about some things. Allow them to make
decisions in those areas.

7

★ ★ ★ 12 ★ ★ ★

Effective reading involves knowing what to
read as well as how to read it. Just because
there's information available to you doesn't mean
that you need it.

8

★ ★ ★ 13 ★ ★ ★

In design work, always keep your drafts.
You may need to refer to a portion of your earlier
work. This prevents having to start
again from scratch.

* * * 14 * * *

Read only the business and trade publications
that give you the greatest value for the amount
of time you spend reading.

* * * 15 * * *

When using equipment that you don't
understand completely, review the manual.
Take the time to learn how to use all the features.
New technology is worth the price only if it is
used efficiently.

9

★ ★ ★ 16 ★ ★ ★

When approving someone else's writing,
don't correct for style, only correct for content.

★ ★ ★ 17 ★ ★ ★

For large projects, identify interim due dates
and measure progress against these newer,
shorter, smaller and easier targets.

10

★ ★ ★ 18 ★ ★ ★

If you drive to work, learn all the
alternate routes.

★ ★ ★ 19 ★ ★ ★

Admit mistakes, especially to colleagues.
It's simply faster than the alternative.

★ ★ ★ 20 ★ ★ ★

Use colored paper to distinguish copies or
drafts from the original.

* * * 21 * * *

12

Have fewer things and see each
of them better.

* * * 22 * * *

When working on the computer, save the document you're working on frequently.

* * * 23 * * *

When you can't figure out the software, ask for help.

13

★ ★ ★ 24 ★ ★ ★

Allocate a few minutes at the end of each day
to put away papers and clear your desk.
Make a list of tomorrow's high priority items.

★ ★ ★ 25 ★ ★ ★

Always carry two batteries for your laptop.
Often there is no plug handy.

14

★ ★ ★ 26 ★ ★ ★

Scheduling regular, short status staff meetings
once a week will increase productivity
and reduce the number of "quick question"
interruptions.

15

★ ★ ★ 27 ★ ★ ★

Learn when to stop gathering facts.
Gather enough information to make a sound
decision, not *all* of the possible information.

* * * 28 * * *

Use a consistent labeling and filing system
so everyone can retrieve information quickly.

* * * 29 * * *

16

Prepare directions to your office or meeting
area and include your phone number.
Always enclose them with each piece of
correspondence when appropriate.

★ ★ ★ 30 ★ ★ ★

Always look at your schedule before agreeing
to accept new work or responsibilities.

★ ★ ★ 31 ★ ★ ★

Separate the good things from the
great things. Don't let the "good"
get in the way of the "great."

17

★ ★ ★ 32 ★ ★ ★

18

When meeting with busy people,
ask for the first appointment
of the day.
Your chances of having to wait
are reduced.

★ ★ ★ 33 ★ ★ ★

Empty spaces are peaceful to look at and live
with. Cleared areas leave your mind free to
think creative or idle thoughts.

★ ★ ★ 34 ★ ★ ★

Anything worth doing is going to
take longer than you think. Allow yourself
some extra time.

★ ★ ★ 35 ★ ★ ★

When traveling, layovers and flight delays are
endemic. Many airports offer services that help
you use that time productively. They provide
space where you can find a desk, telex,
telephone, fax and sometimes, even secretaries.

★ ★ ★ 36 ★ ★ ★

Avoid booking the last flight of the day.
If it is canceled for some reason,
you're stranded overnight.

20

★ ★ ★ 37 ★ ★ ★

Calculate the value of your time. It may be
cheaper to use a vendor than to make it or
fix it yourself.

★ ★ ★ 38 ★ ★ ★

Set aside time every week for important
priorities that require blocks of creative time.

21

★ ★ ★ 39 ★ ★ ★

If you're in the office extremely early or
extremely late—before or after business hours—
and the phone rings, don't answer it.

★ ★ ★ 40 ★ ★ ★

Always invest in people. Train your staff well
and continually.

★ ★ ★ 41 ★ ★ ★

Write instructions for frequently used processes or procedures. It saves everyone time, particularly new employees.

★ ★ ★ 42 ★ ★ ★

Keep procedural manuals, flowcharts, timelines and instructions up-to-date.

23

$\star\star\star$ 43 $\star\star\star$

Be proud that you found time for
a break and still got done what
needed to be done. Don't be proud
because you haven't enjoyed a
weekend break in three months.

24

★ ★ ★ 44 ★ ★ ★

Before purchasing a computer and software, identify your true needs and the tasks you will be doing. Learn the differences between word processing, a page-layout program, a database program and a spreadsheet; then select the most appropriate hardware and software.

★ ★ ★ 45 ★ ★ ★

Always keep your tickets in the same place.

25

★ ★ ★ 46 ★ ★ ★

Use it or lose it. Before increasing your space,
organize. Weed out unnecessary, unneeded and
unwanted items from your office.

★ ★ ★ 47 ★ ★ ★

Before telephoning, write down points you
intend to cover. Plan your message, particularly
now that voice mail is so prevalent.

26

★ ★ ★ 48 ★ ★ ★

Beware of gifts you receive from suppliers.
They clutter your work environment. Only keep
the ones you use or find attractive.

★ ★ ★ 49 ★ ★ ★

27

Separate bills from incoming money.
Deposit the money immediately;
the bills can wait.

★ ★ ★ 50 ★ ★ ★

Learn when to stop working.

★ ★ ★ 51 ★ ★ ★

Set up binders for commonly sought materials.
You will avoid sorting through files to
retrieve the answers to frequently asked
questions. You will also alleviate the need to
circulate copies to everyone.

28

★ ★ ★ 52 ★ ★ ★

When traveling, dictate letters and mail work
back to the office. Carry along prestamped,
padded envelopes. When you return to the
office, the letters have already gone out and what
is waiting on your return is the reply.

29

★ ★ ★ 53 ★ ★ ★

Choose work that is in harmony with your
values, beliefs and interests.

★ ★ ★ 54 ★ ★ ★

If the software program you have now works
perfectly well, do not upgrade it just because a
new version is released.

★ ★ ★ 55 ★ ★ ★

Beware the seductiveness of easy-to-do and
less-important tasks. Start every day with the
most important thing you have to do.

30

★ ★ ★ 56 ★ ★ ★

Break the habit of writing things on numerous
scraps of paper or sticky note pads. Write notes
in the appropriate place the first time.

★ ★ ★ 57 ★ ★ ★

Build routine activities into your weekly pattern
of life. Back up your computer every Friday, clean
your in-box twice each day, check with staff
every Monday morning.

31

★ ★ ★ 58 ★ ★ ★

Buy greeting cards in advance for unexpected
occasions—humorous, get well, thank you,
congratulations and sympathy cards.
Buy birthday cards for the entire year.

32

★ ★ ★ 59 ★ ★ ★

Set up telephone appointments just as you
would schedule in-person appointments.

★ ★ ★ 60 ★ ★ ★

Always, always, always keep the big picture in
mind. It makes choosing so much easier.

★ ★ ★ 61 ★ ★ ★

Set your own daily, weekly and monthly goals.
Make sure you do some activity every day
that leads you toward your goals.

33

★ ★ ★ 62 ★ ★ ★

Buy in bulk. Whether you're getting office
supplies, appreciation gifts or cards, it's more
efficient to buy for long-range needs than to
frequently run out to buy individual items.

34

★ ★ ★ 63 ★ ★ ★

Always place the most recent correspondence
in the front of the file.

★ ★ ★ 64 ★ ★ ★

At the end of each day, prepare for the next
by pulling all the client files or appointment
information that you will need.

★ ★ ★ 65 ★ ★ ★

Cancel or bow out of as many unnecessary
meetings as you can.

35

★ ★ ★ 66 ★ ★ ★

Beware of technology that overcomplicates.
When there are too many communication
channels—voice mail, electronic mail,
central message center, interoffice mail—
it can be confusing and information
can be overlooked.

★ ★ ★ 67 ★ ★ ★

Learn to ask for help.

36

★ ★ ★ 68 ★ ★ ★

Rather than hiring a permanent staff person,
consider hiring a series of student interns.
They are generally enthusiastic, energetic
and eager to learn.

★ ★ ★ 69 ★ ★ ★

Carpool or take public transportation to work.

37

★ ★ ★ 70 ★ ★ ★

Celebrate your accomplishments.
On your way home, reflect on the exact tasks
that you completed during the day.

★ ★ ★ 71 ★ ★ ★

If you must leave something uncompleted
at the end of the day, make sure it is a
low priority item.

38

★ ★ ★ 72 ★ ★ ★

Certain key information should be in more
than one place. In addition to addresses, use your
Rolodex for recording odd bits of information,
such as Social Security numbers,
your federal ID number, lock combinations
and your driver's license number.

39

★ ★ ★ 73 ★ ★ ★

Telecommuting is possible; it just takes
planning and thought.

★★★ 74 ★★★

Change your computer password every month.

★★★ 75 ★★★

Don't store the password in an
easy-to-find location.

40

★★★ 76 ★★★

Don't choose a password that is easy to guess.
If you mix numbers and letters together in your
password, it is very difficult to access.

★ ★ ★ 77 ★ ★ ★

Always leave your telephone number when
leaving a message, even if you think the
receiver has it.

★ ★ ★ 78 ★ ★ ★

Change your voice mail message every day.
Let people know your schedule and when they
can expect a call back.

41

★ ★ ★ 79 ★ ★ ★

Checklists are great time-savers. Keep them
for packing, traveling, moving, filling orders or
any repeated office task.

★ ★ ★ 80 ★ ★ ★

In any planning session, define the problem
first and clarify the parameters before you
attempt to solve it.

42

★ ★ ★ 81 ★ ★ ★

Avoid leaving things out as reminders;
they create piles and clutter. Put each item away
and jot a note on your calendar or on your
to-do list so that you will not forget.

43

★ ★ ★ 82 ★ ★ ★

Circle or highlight phone numbers the first time
you look up each number in the telephone
directory. You are very likely to need it again.

★★★ 83 ★★★

Simplify decision making by
making routine decisions routine.
When you have to make the same
decision multiple times,
you actually need a rule,
not another decision.

44

★★★ 84 ★★★

Conduct a companywide forms-and-reports
audit with the goal to reduce as many of them
as possible.

★★★ 85 ★★★

Print out a hard copy of the directory that
lists the files on your hard drive. It helps others
find things.

45

★ ★ ★ 86 ★ ★ ★

Consider faxing routine material after hours,
late in the evening or early in the morning,
when phone rates are lower and fax machines
are less likely to be busy. Never call to
see if your fax arrived.

46

★ ★ ★ 87 ★ ★ ★

Color-code computer disks for easier and faster
identification.

★ ★ ★ 88 ★ ★ ★

Avoid nonspecific file labels such as "general,"
"miscellaneous," "information," "pending" or
"interesting stuff."

★ ★ ★ 89 ★ ★ ★

47

Consolidate similar activities such as
telephone calls, correspondence or errands and
do them together.

⋆ ⋆ ⋆ 90 ⋆ ⋆ ⋆

Continually look for ways to improve. Small steps add up; changes need not be large to be significant. Periodically check to see if all the tasks and projects on your list really need to be done. Drop those that don't.

⋆ ⋆ ⋆ 91 ⋆ ⋆ ⋆

Open your mail near a wastebasket. Place junk mail in it without opening.

48

* * * 92 * * *

Particularly if you have a home office,
keep your personal and business papers separate.

* * * 93 * * *

Pay bills the 1st and the 15th of each
month only.

49

★ ★ ★ 94 ★ ★ ★

Place office equipment strategically;
consider ease of use, minimizing steps and
reducing distractions.

★ ★ ★ 95 ★ ★ ★

Playing with the computer, tinkering with
fonts and formatting documents can take an
extraordinary amount of time. Always keep the
results in mind.

★ ★ ★ 96 ★ ★ ★

Coordinate outgoing mail. Many times,
offices send overnight and express packages
to the same address on the same day. Work with
coworkers to see if some mail can be bunched
to save money.

51

★ ★ ★ 97 ★ ★ ★

Back up computer files before you do any
installation of software or hardware.

★★★ 98 ★★★

To streamline life on the road, choose rental companies that give you priority treatment when you need a vehicle. Check hotels for frequent-stay discounts and always inquire about corporate rates.

★★★ 99 ★★★

Check electronic mail at least once each day. For ease, tie this habit to some other ritual you do regularly.

52

* * * 100 * * *

Create an easy-to-fill-out fax cover sheet to go
with your documents.

* * * 101 * * *

Avoid those plastic-bound card cases.
If people move or you have new cards to add,
it's impossible to alphabetize the cards without
removing each one.

53

★ ★ ★ 102 ★ ★ ★

Crises always occur.
Have good contingency plans.

★ ★ ★ 103 ★ ★ ★

54

Develop a personal information handling system
and a basic organizational style that works for
you and that you can live with, not necessarily
what others think you should use.

★ ★ ★   104   ★ ★ ★

Delegate the summarizing of reading materials
among colleagues. Everyone stays better
informed, while each person, overall,
spends less time reading.

55

★ ★ ★   105   ★ ★ ★

Don't bother to proofread a phone number.
Call it to be sure it's right.

★ ★ ★ 106 ★ ★ ★

Develop a form that you can easily fax back
for routine inquiries. Include your name,
title and the answers to key questions
callers frequently ask.

★ ★ ★ 107 ★ ★ ★

Do as much research as possible online. It is
faster than a manual library search.

★ ★ ★ 108 ★ ★ ★

Consider adjustments that are made to work
loads when staff members take vacations.
Could some of the approaches used during
holiday periods be extended throughout the year
for greater effectiveness?

57

★ ★ ★ 109 ★ ★ ★

Date and make notations on all paperwork as
completed. Indicate any actions taken.

★★★ 110 ★★★

Create a system for manual bill paying. When a bill
arrives, open it, place it in the mailing envelope,
stamp it and add the return address label. Note the
due date on the outside of the envelope and put it in
a tickler file. At bill-paying time, write the check,
enter it into the ledger, file the receipt and mail it.

★★★ 111 ★★★

Dictate your correspondence.
It is faster than writing.

★ ★ ★ 112 ★ ★ ★

Divide your task list into two columns:
one for short-term activities and one for
long-term projects.

★ ★ ★ 113 ★ ★ ★

59

Do one thing at a time. When you're finished,
move on to the next item.

★ ★ ★ 114 ★ ★ ★

Don't trust your memory. Always write it down.

★ ★ ★ 115 ★ ★ ★

Design a phone interview sheet for gathering
information from potential clients who call you.
List name, address, home and work phone
numbers along with some pertinent questions to
ask to help you evaluate their needs. This is an
excellent prompt when you get an unexpected
call and your mind is elsewhere.

★ ★ ★ 116 ★ ★ ★

Keep duplicates of equipment and supplies in
all the locations where you regularly reach for a
staple remover, three-hole punch, scissors
or highlighter.

61

★ ★ ★ 117 ★ ★ ★

Crises are often caused by shortsightedness.
Plan regularly both short term and long term.

*** 118 ***

Learn when to say "no." You can't make everyone
like you, nor satisfy all their needs.

*** 119 ***

When saying "no," be firm without apology,
undue explanation or guilt.

62

★ ★ ★ 120 ★ ★ ★

Say "I don't know," when you don't.

★ ★ ★ 121 ★ ★ ★

Develop routines to simplify and handle the
mundane chores of your work. Find ways to
eliminate as much bureaucracy as possible.

63

* * * 122 * * *

Don't procrastinate. Do what needs to be done
in a timely manner.

* * * 123 * * *

Create a standard letter to send to companies
that ship you unwanted catalogs. Attach your
mailing label and send it to them.

64

★ ★ ★ 124 ★ ★ ★

Choose the most appropriate avenue for
communications. Consider the receiver,
the subject and your desired outcome.

★ ★ ★ 125 ★ ★ ★

65

Delay is rarely beneficial. Recognize the
greater unpleasantness, work, money, time and
stress that result from postponing a decision.

★★★ 126 ★★★

Don't create more information than you really need. Where a 2-page proposal would have been fine, now a 12-page proposal with charts and graphs can blossom.

★★★ 127 ★★★

Encourage others to take risks and stretch beyond their current capabilities. The whole department will thrive.

* * * 128 * * *

Be willing to accept a temporary
inconvenience if it will result in a
permanent improvement.

67

★ ★ ★ 129 ★ ★ ★

Always double-check that days and dates
match up. Is Wednesday, July 10th,
really on a Wednesday?

★ ★ ★ 130 ★ ★ ★

Each day back up any data or applications
you've modified that day.

68

★ ★ ★ 131 ★ ★ ★

Find out what people do well and find ways to
let them do more of it.

★ ★ ★ 132 ★ ★ ★

People do not change their core natures, even
with training. Don't try to teach a pig to sing. It
frustrates you and annoys the pig.

★ ★ ★ 133 ★ ★ ★

Eighty percent of the value comes from
20 percent of the things you do. Focus on the
valued few, not the trivial many.

★ ★ ★ 134 ★ ★ ★

Establish times when you will take phone calls
and save your return calls for a block of time.

★ ★ ★ 135 ★ ★ ★

Even electronic mail messages take up space.
Resist the temptation to send messages for
everyone's FYI. Consider the time the recipient
has to spend reading, sorting, filing and/or
dumping it.

71

★ ★ ★ 136 ★ ★ ★

Be aware of the realities of cost and effort.
Going the cheap route is often more expensive.

★ ★ ★ 137 ★ ★ ★

When traveling, try not to depart or arrive
during rush hour, when your chances of being
late due to traffic increase.

★ ★ ★ 138 ★ ★ ★

Get your seat assignment and boarding pass
in advance so you can proceed directly to
the boarding area.

72

* * * 139 * * *

Excluding true life-and-death situations,
nothing is as important as it first seems.

* * * 140 * * *

File the important things, but file them daily.

73

★ ★ ★ 141 ★ ★ ★

Focus. It's easier to do 100 things toward a
common goal than 50 things toward
50 separate goals.

74

★ ★ ★ 142 ★ ★ ★

For important reports and memos,
have somebody else proofread the document.

★ ★ ★ 143 ★ ★ ★

Don't trust the spell-check function in
your computer.

★ ★ ★ 144 ★ ★ ★

Use drop-off and delivery services as much
as possible. When you add up the time it would
take for you to pay the toll, park the car,
deliver the document and return to pick it up,
it's probably more expensive than having
the vendor come to you.

75

★ ★ ★ 145 ★ ★ ★

Always add at least an hour each day to your
schedule for interruptions from phone calls,
unplanned meetings, questions, searching and
other time-robbers that are unavoidable.

76

★ ★ ★ 146 ★ ★ ★

When you are out in the field, remember to
bring all your tools. When you only take a
selection, you will invariably need one
you don't have.

★ ★ ★ 147 ★ ★ ★

Forms are useful to track such things as
work flow, projects, responsibilities, schedules
and personnel. They help simplify
communications. Make sure they are well
designed, clear and concise.

77

★ ★ ★ 148 ★ ★ ★

Grief over past mistakes is unproductive.
Learn the lesson and move on.

★ ★ ★ 149 ★ ★ ★

Handwrite thank you notes for people who have
helped you. That small kindness will
reap great rewards.

★ ★ ★ 150 ★ ★ ★

Handle mail only once and move it on.
Either delegate, read, act on, file or toss it the
first time you touch it.

★★★ 151 ★★★

Have two rotating sets of complete backup
disks, with the most current set off-site, at home
or at a client's site. As soon as you make your
most up-to-date backup, take it off-site and bring
the older backup back in for recycling.

79

★★★ 152 ★★★

When you need professional advice,
get it from professionals, not from your friends.

★★★ 153 ★★★

Be sure that a computer will actually help
simplify your life and not overly complicate it.
The key to making electronic technology save
time for you is to be selective about how much
time you devote to that technology.

80

★★★ 154 ★★★

Don't accept a task until you understand the
"why" of it, not just the "what" of it.

★ ★ ★ 155 ★ ★ ★

Have as many of your monthly bills as you can
converted to automatic payments by your bank.
This eliminates paperwork and will save you in
postage, costs and frequent trips to the post
office for supplies.

81

★ ★ ★ 156 ★ ★ ★

Have only one project or file open on your desk
at any time.

★ ★ ★ 157 ★ ★ ★

Question "common practice." Pay attention to
tasks that are delegated to you or that you assign
to others. What is the reason for the job in
question? How important is it? Who actually
looks at this information?

★ ★ ★ 158 ★ ★ ★

Hire people smarter than you, with talents in
different areas, and let them shine.

★★★ 159 ★★★

When your calls are returned, note the time the call was placed. In the future, that is usually the best time to reach the caller.

★★★ 160 ★★★

Hold meetings at 8 AM, 11 AM or 4 PM to avoid breaking up prime work time.

★ ★ ★ 161 ★ ★ ★

Honor your own past experience.
Become comfortable in saying "no" to people,
tasks and opportunities that take you off track.

84

★ ★ ★ 162 ★ ★ ★

If you can't find the time to learn how to use a
computer, don't buy it unless you're going to
assign its operation to a staff person.

★ ★ ★ 163 ★ ★ ★

Don't overbook yourself by overscheduling
your activities.

★ ★ ★ 164 ★ ★ ★

If you conduct much business by telephone,
consider special equipment such as a headset
and automatic dialer or a speaker phone to
increase efficiency. These devices make long
periods on the phone less stressful, and your
hands will be free to take notes.

85

★★★ 165 ★★★

Don't risk spending time and effort needlessly.
Ask your boss for direction on assignments and
for clarification when needed. Don't guess.

★★★ 166 ★★★

Learn to end phone conversations firmly
but gracefully.

★★★ 167 ★★★

In large companies, let a recipient know
a fax is coming. Most fax machines are not in
sight of the recipient.

★★★ 168 ★★★

Instead of parking your car at the airport,
consider taking a cab, shuttle or limo. They are
more convenient and often less expensive.

★ ★ ★ 169 ★ ★ ★

In all things, keep it simple.

88

★ ★ ★ 170 ★ ★ ★

Investigate computer programs that automate
the invoicing, bill-paying and
financial-report-generation process.

★ ★ ★ 171 ★ ★ ★

Keep a diary of your accomplishments at work.
Then when you ask for a raise, you'll have the
information you need to back it up.

★ ★ ★ 172 ★ ★ ★

Hold a meeting because it is needed,
not because it is Tuesday.

★ ★ ★ 173 ★ ★ ★

Invite only those who have direct responsibility
for the items or actions to be discussed at the
meeting. The fewer the people, the faster the
meeting will go.

★ ★ ★ 174 ★ ★ ★

If it is a choice between a letter and a
telephone call, call.

★ ★ ★ 175 ★ ★ ★

Don't add unless you subtract.
Volunteer to do something only after you
give up something else.

★ ★ ★ 176 ★ ★ ★

Keep your job and your life in perspective.
Success at the expense of relaxation and
enjoyment is no success.

92

★ ★ ★ 177 ★ ★ ★

Delegate more. It extends results from what you
can do to what you can control. It also increases
the satisfaction others feel in their work.

★ ★ ★ 178 ★ ★ ★

Keep a copy of your warranty or repair
information in your tickler file on the anniversary
of purchase dates. Once a year, most warranties
are up for review, and routine service calls
can be placed at that time also.

93

★ ★ ★ 179 ★ ★ ★

Label everything: binders, books,
folders, suitcases.

★ ★ ★ 180 ★ ★ ★

Ask listeners to repeat their understanding
of your directions. Less time is spent
repeating directions than redoing an
incorrect task or project.

★ ★ ★ 181 ★ ★ ★

At a trade show, instead of carrying all the
literature you collect, mail it back to your office.
Take along a preaddressed and stamped
envelope for this purpose.

94

★ ★ ★ 182 ★ ★ ★

Learn to appreciate different approaches.
Different does not mean wrong or inferior;
it only means different.

★ ★ ★ 183 ★ ★ ★

95

Don't automatically print a hard copy of each of
your e-mail messages. Set up and use effective
electronic filing systems.

* * * 184 * * *

Always leave your full name with
your telephone message.
The recipient may know more than
one Jose, Mary, Quan or Vicki.

96

★ ★ ★ 185 ★ ★ ★

Learn how to use all of the functions on
your telephone, not just the "hold" and
"send" buttons.

★ ★ ★ 186 ★ ★ ★

97

When you move, tape your business card to
your new phone. Your new address, phone and
fax numbers will be at your fingertips.

187

Don't buy a computer because it is fashionable or stylish. A computer does not supply you with knowledge or common sense.

188

Be cautious about buying the most powerful and comprehensive version of either hardware or software. Consider the importance of ease of use.

✦ ✦ ✦ 189 ✦ ✦ ✦

Get your priorities straight.
Looking back, no one ever wished
that he or she had returned
more phone calls or attended
more meetings.

99

★ ★ ★ 190 ★ ★ ★

Keep your desk and work area neat.

★ ★ ★ 191 ★ ★ ★

Leave concise phone mail messages.
Let people you call know when you will be
available for their return call and always tell
them what it is concerning.

* * * 192 * * *

Link a hard-to-remember activity to a strongly
established habit; for example, when you change
to daylight savings time, check the charge on
your fire extinguisher.

101

* * * 193 * * *

Limit your reading material. Realize that
you can't read, know or retain all the information
you receive.

★ ★ ★ 194 ★ ★ ★

Let your assistant help you get and
stay organized.

★ ★ ★ 195 ★ ★ ★

List all frequent flyer numbers and hotel
special guest numbers on a sheet of paper,
reduce it and carry it in your wallet.
Eliminate the need to carry individual cards and
prevent having to call later to get credit for the
stay or for the trip.

★ ★ ★ 196 ★ ★ ★

List the most unpleasant task as your first
chore of the day, then do it.

★ ★ ★ 197 ★ ★ ★

Locate the switch for the visual or audible alarms
that indicate you have just received more mail
online. Turn it off during those times when you
don't want to be interrupted.

103

★★★ 198 ★★★

Look for better ways of doing things. You can buy stamps through the mail as well as by phone. Banking by mail is timely and efficient.

★★★ 199 ★★★

Use a virus scanning program to protect your computer whenever you bring in other disks that are not packaged software.

★ ★ ★ 200 ★ ★ ★

When your computer hardware or software
doesn't work, before calling the
800 support number, return it to the store
where you purchased it. It's often quicker.

105

★ ★ ★ 201 ★ ★ ★

Recognize when to stop creating drafts. It's
probably not getting any better, just different.

★ ★ ★ 202 ★ ★ ★

Make a list of all the projects, tasks and items
you have been procrastinating about. Re-evaluate
each of them. Make a decision and do it.

★ ★ ★ 203 ★ ★ ★

Don't expect any product to organize you.
You have to do the work.

106

★ ★ ★ 204 ★ ★ ★

On your way home from work, select a spot
along the highway. In your imagination, dump
each day's stresses at that same spot.

★ ★ ★ 205 ★ ★ ★

Keep your filing system easy to use and
to understand.

107

★ ★ ★ 206 ★ ★ ★

Learn when to say "no" to a potential client.
Refer him or her to a colleague.

★ ★ ★ 207 ★ ★ ★

Make sharing of electronic data easier
by choosing software that clients,
coworkers or associates already use. It makes
getting help easier.

108

*** 208 ***

Make a conscious, concerted effort
to do less.

109

★ ★ ★ 209 ★ ★ ★

Learn your e-mail software system thoroughly
and customize it for your use. Learn,
for example, how to set up distribution lists for
convenient group mailing to work teams.

★ ★ ★ 210 ★ ★ ★

Make sure phone and extension numbers are
on all interoffice memos. It will save everyone
time when searching for your number.

110

★★★ 211 ★★★

If your flight is canceled or
delayed, don't stand in line.
Go directly to a phone
and call the reservations line
to make your change.

111

★ ★ ★ 212 ★ ★ ★

Make your environment conducive to working.
Choose an office space and an office layout that
you enjoy. Remove all distractions.

★ ★ ★ 213 ★ ★ ★

Many hotels will extend your checkout time
if you request it in the morning. If your meeting
runs until checkout time, this extra hour or
so will make packing up and concluding your
business much calmer.

★ ★ ★ 214 ★ ★ ★

Learn when to let go and walk away.

★ ★ ★ 215 ★ ★ ★

Use a sign that you can place on your door,
on your desk or on the wall next to your cubicle
to communicate to people when you
cannot be disturbed.

113

★ ★ ★ 216 ★ ★ ★

Many publications offer the alternative of
receiving disks instead of the magazine.
This can sometimes be useful.

★ ★ ★ 217 ★ ★ ★

Use electronic mail whenever possible. It is
particularly helpful for telecommuters.

★ ★ ★ 218 ★ ★ ★

Use luggage that has wheels.

★ ★ ★ 219 ★ ★ ★

Never check luggage. You can live for a week
out of a single carryon.

115

★ ★ ★ 220 ★ ★ ★

For various multistep projects that carry
separate time lines, create a master list by
integrating all the project deadlines to create a
master monthly task sheet.

116

★ ★ ★ 221 ★ ★ ★

Never accept a phone call when you're in
a face-to-face meeting; it's rude.

* * * 222 * * *

Move closer to your work to cut down
commute time.

* * * 223 * * *

Meetings are very expensive. Consider these
alternatives: a memo to make the announcement,
a request for information sent via e-mail, a
telephone conference call or video conferencing.

117

★ ★ ★ 224 ★ ★ ★

Use only one calendar or planning system
that includes your personal as well as
business appointments.

★ ★ ★ 225 ★ ★ ★

Don't confuse long hours with productivity;
they are not synonymous.

118

★ ★ ★ 226 ★ ★ ★

Never get up to make a single photocopy.
Take items to the photocopier when you have
a number of things to copy and do them
all at the same time.

119

★ ★ ★ 227 ★ ★ ★

Learn to recognize the inconsequential,
then ignore it.

*** 228 ***

If, knowing what you know now, you would not
have gotten involved in a particular activity,
begin to look for ways to drop it.

*** 229 ***

Make a to-do list every day. Keep it where you
can see it and set priorities on the list.

★ ★ ★ 230 ★ ★ ★

Don't agonize over minor
decisions; they're still minor with
or without the agony.

121

★★★ 231 ★★★

Never write down a phone number without
the person's name.

★★★ 232 ★★★

Once your backup exceeds ten floppy disks,
investigate a higher capacity disk or tape drive or
other media. They are faster and safer.

* * * 233 * * *

Use only one telephone and address book.
Carry telephone numbers with you all the time.

* * * 234 * * *

Keep a backup copy of your address and
telephone book.

★ ★ ★ 235 ★ ★ ★

Make decisions in a timely fashion.
Rarely does waiting significantly improve the
quality of the decision.

★ ★ ★ 236 ★ ★ ★

Prioritize your list of things to do for the
day with an A for the most important ones,
B for the next most important and
C for the least important. No more than
20 percent should be As.

★ ★ ★ 237 ★ ★ ★

Purge your files annually. Place a discard date
on the document when you file it to make the
purging process go faster.

★ ★ ★ 238 ★ ★ ★

When you receive a publication, scan the title
page or skim the table of contents, identify the
articles that are of interest to you, tear them
out and toss the publication.

125

★ ★ ★ 239 ★ ★ ★

Get rid of "stuff." The less you have,
the less you have to care for.

★ ★ ★ 240 ★ ★ ★

To save storage space, consider archiving some
of your paper records. Electronic storage takes
less space than a paper document and can
sometimes be easier to access.

126

★ ★ ★ 241 ★ ★ ★

When flying, make sure that any writing utensil
you carry can adjust to fluctuations of altitude.
Avoid fountain pens or refillable piston pens.
They will invariably leak or explode at the worst
possible time. Never carry them in your pockets.

★ ★ ★ 242 ★ ★ ★

Put things back where they belong as soon
as possible.

*** 243 ***

Periodically sort your computer files by date.
Review anything that is one year old. Either toss
it or transfer it to a floppy disk for storage.

*** 244 ***

Learn the difference between urgent and
important. Urgent things nag at you loudly, but
they may not be genuinely important. Important
items may be continually delayed because they
don't make much noise.

★ ★ ★ 245 ★ ★ ★

Put papers away after you use them.
This reduces the likelihood of stray papers
becoming attached to the incorrect document
and being misfiled.

129

★ ★ ★ 246 ★ ★ ★

Slow down and do it right the first time so that
you don't have to do it over again later.

★ ★ ★ 247 ★ ★ ★

Use small personalized return address stickers for many purposes such as getting film developed, signing up at registration tables and updating directories. Carry them with you and keep a supply in your desk.

★ ★ ★ 248 ★ ★ ★

Put your address inside your luggage as well as on the outside.

130

★ ★ ★ 249 ★ ★ ★

All computers are not the same. For the money
you will be paying and the time commitment
involved, make sure you take them out for a test
drive before purchasing.

131

★ ★ ★ 250 ★ ★ ★

Take samples of your real work with you
before you buy.

★ ★ ★ 251 ★ ★ ★

Regard the telephone as a servant,
not as a tyrant that must be obeyed
or answered. It is there for your convenience,
not the caller's. Ignore it completely if you are
engaged in a task that requires full concentration
or is more important.

★ ★ ★ 252 ★ ★ ★

Rent a postage machine and scale.
Don't bother with paper stamps.

★ ★ ★ 253 ★ ★ ★

When you're faced with a problem,
before trying to solve it, take five minutes to
think it through. Then make a reasoned decision
and respond.

133

★ ★ ★ 254 ★ ★ ★

Keep track of business expenses as they accrue,
so that your monthly expense report is not so
onerous to complete.

★ ★ ★ 255 ★ ★ ★

Resist telling people all the details about how to do something. Instead, tell them what needs to be done and the results desired. Allow them to choose the method.

★ ★ ★ 256 ★ ★ ★

Make sure you schedule time on your calendar each week for office maintenance. Take time to straighten up and keep things organized.

134

★★★ 257 ★★★

Use toll-free numbers as much as possible. The toll-free information number is 800-555-1212.

★★★ 258 ★★★

Resist the free or cheap subscriptions for things that you won't read or that don't contain much good information.

135

★ ★ ★ 259 ★ ★ ★

Once your "things to read" stack becomes six months old, throw it away.

★ ★ ★ 260 ★ ★ ★

Reward employees for reducing paperwork. Publicize the names and praise the managers who cure their departments of excessive bureaucratic procedures and forms.

★ ★ ★ 261 ★ ★ ★

Schedule multiple out-of-the-office
appointments for the same day instead of
spreading them throughout the week.
This reduces your travel time and your
parking hassles.

137

★ ★ ★ 262 ★ ★ ★

When only a brief reply is needed,
return the original letter with your notation
added to the bottom.

★ ★ ★ 263 ★ ★ ★

Keep things close to where you will be
using them. Divide and store paper, supplies and
materials in easy-to-use locations.

★ ★ ★ 264 ★ ★ ★

Run an optimizing program once each quarter
for routine maintenance of your computer.

138

* * * 265 * * *

To identify files to remove from your hard drive,
sort your files differently—by size or date or
function.

* * * 266 * * *

139

Save travel lists you make up prior to a trip.
Shortly, you will have a fairly foolproof list to
help you minimize stress and maximize
effectiveness.

* * * 267 * * *

Have your car serviced while you are
away on a trip.

* * * 268 * * *

Encourage employees, particularly new ones,
to question activities that seem unnecessary or
procedures that seem unduly complicated.
A fresh pair of eyes often sees more clearly
than the experienced.

★ ★ ★ 269 ★ ★ ★

Say "no" to things, places, people, tasks and
opportunities that clutter up your life.

★ ★ ★ 270 ★ ★ ★

Schedule complex or intense tasks during peak
energy times and mechanical, automatic tasks
during lower energy times.

141

★ ★ ★ 271 ★ ★ ★

Use a travel agent. It costs no more and saves
time and effort.

★ ★ ★ 272 ★ ★ ★

142

Take as much time as you need to find a great
travel agent and keep him or her forever.

* * * 273 * * *

Only take on what you are able to do.

* * * 274 * * *

Seek to simplify processes, procedures and
policies that are too complicated.

143

* * * 275 * * *

Clear your desk at the end of each day, even if
you're in a busy period.

★ ★ ★ 276 ★ ★ ★

Keep overhead low. It's not what you make, it's
what you keep that matters.

★ ★ ★ 277 ★ ★ ★

Separate the computer applications from the
data files you create. When you back up your
documents, don't bother to back up your
application programs each time.

144

⋆ ⋆ ⋆ 278 ⋆ ⋆ ⋆

Before the final product goes to the client or customer, be sure that another pair of eyes reviews it.

⋆ ⋆ ⋆ 279 ⋆ ⋆ ⋆

145

Set aside quiet time each day for concentrated work. Always honor this commitment.

★★★ 280 ★★★

Only keep the business cards that you asked for or are interested in. Just because people give you their cards doesn't mean you have to keep them.

146

★★★ 281 ★★★

Organize all your business cards in a single location, either on a computer or in a Rolodex, but not in various stacks in various places in your desk.

★ ★ ★ 282 ★ ★ ★

Always provide people the training, supplies and
tools they need to complete a job successfully.

★ ★ ★ 283 ★ ★ ★

For long documents, include a one-page
summary of your major points and conclusions.

147

★ ★ ★ 284 ★ ★ ★

If you haven't read the last four issues of a
magazine, it is time to end your subscription.

★ ★ ★ 285 ★ ★ ★

Use vendors as much as possible. Employees
add an extra level of complexity, cost,
management and time.

148

★ ★ ★ 286 ★ ★ ★

Schedule a time each day to work on your mail.
It could be 15 minutes or a half hour,
but do it every day.

★ ★ ★ 287 ★ ★ ★

Simplify your electronic needs. Be cautious if
you have a tendency to want the latest, greatest,
newest addition. You can spend more time
buying, installing and learning to use the new
toy than actually being productive.

★ ★ ★ 288 ★ ★ ★

Set more realistic time frames for the completion of projects. Not everything needs to be done today.

150

★ ★ ★ 289 ★ ★ ★

Create standard documents and templates whenever possible.

★ ★ ★ 290 ★ ★ ★

Keep extra manila file folders close at hand.
Create a new file as soon as you get paperwork
related to a new project.

★ ★ ★ 291 ★ ★ ★

151

Use your time effectively. That includes
allowing time for thinking and
even daydreaming.

* * * 292 * * *

Simplifying your work
is important.
Simplifying everyone's work
is even more so.

152

★ ★ ★ 293 ★ ★ ★

Slow down a little. Rushing begets rushing.

★ ★ ★ 294 ★ ★ ★

Get out all the materials necessary to complete
a job before you start.

153

★ ★ ★ 295 ★ ★ ★

Color-code your files.

★ ★ ★ 296 ★ ★ ★

Speak and write concisely, simply and directly.
Avoid jargon, acronyms and technical terms.

154

★★★ 297 ★★★

Stamp "no reply necessary" on as much of your
outgoing correspondence as possible.

★★★ 298 ★★★

Use waiting time to read, plan, study,
review or write.

155

★ ★ ★ 299 ★ ★ ★

Stop postponing decisions about small problems;
they'll simply turn into large ones later.

★ ★ ★ 300 ★ ★ ★

Combat the perfectionistic tendency. Weigh the
value of real, complete and possibly imperfect
work over late, incomplete but ideal work.

★ ★ ★ 301 ★ ★ ★

Be sure that the container where you store your
spare, off-site backup disks is fireproof.

★ ★ ★ 302 ★ ★ ★

Come into work early and leave early, or
come in later and leave later.
You miss the peak commute rush hours and gain
uninterrupted time.

157

* * * 303 * * *

Keep a list or file folder for each person
with whom you consult frequently. Note items to
be discussed as they come up. When several
items have accumulated, take care of all of
them at once.

* * * 304 * * *

Take yourself less seriously.

158

★ ★ ★ 305 ★ ★ ★

Competency is seductive. Don't spend a lot of
time on things that aren't important just because
you're good at those activities.

★ ★ ★ 306 ★ ★ ★

159

Computer files need to be accessible, up-to-date,
properly categorized and regularly maintained.

* * * 307 * * *

Talk to other people about how they have
simplified their work practices.

* * * 308 * * *

160

Tape-record your correspondence while
commuting. This saves time for you and
your secretary.

★★★ 309 ★★★

The success of a meeting is generally
determined by the work done outside of the
meeting, not by the number of meetings called.

★★★ 310 ★★★

Avoid faxing when regular interoffice mail can
suffice. Sending a fax does not automatically
make your message any more important.
It simply makes it more urgent.

★ ★ ★ 311 ★ ★ ★

When a situation, circumstance or task occurs
more than three times a year, it's time to
systematize it.

★ ★ ★ 312 ★ ★ ★

Take advantage of the time you spend on an
airplane. Planning, editing and reading are ideal
in-flight tasks to do.

★ ★ ★ 313 ★ ★ ★

Throughout the year, collect items that will
help you at budget time. Don't wait until a
couple of weeks before it's due.
Your judgment will suffer.

163

★ ★ ★ 314 ★ ★ ★

To leave an in-house meeting on time,
schedule another appointment or conference call
to begin at the ending time of the meeting.

* * * 315 * * *

Track multiple or large projects on a wall chart.

* * * 316 * * *

If you have magazines in good condition, consider donating them to nursing homes, children's schools, hospitals, clinics or anywhere individuals have to wait for a period of time. Even some nonprofit organizations would appreciate them.

164

★ ★ ★ 317 ★ ★ ★

Establish relationships with reliable vendors.
Evaluate periodically, not every time you need an
item or service.

★ ★ ★ 318 ★ ★ ★

To avoid excess effort, use the expertise of
vendors to help you develop criteria for
equipment or product selection.

165

* * * 319 * * *

Try returning phone calls about ten minutes
before noon and ten minutes before 5 PM. Most
people are in their offices at those times.

* * * 320 * * *

Understand the impact of taxes, inflation,
time and compound interest on your
financial situation.

* * * 321 * * *

Update your database once a week,
no matter what.

* * * 322 * * *

Use simple, plain English. Write with nouns
and strong verbs. Use short sentences and
short paragraphs.

167

★ ★ ★ 323 ★ ★ ★

To reduce telemarketing calls, write to
Telephone Preference Service, c/o the Direct
Marketing Association, P.O. Box 9014,
Farmingdale, NY 11735-9014. Include your
name, address and complete telephone number.

★ ★ ★ 324 ★ ★ ★

Learn to ask, "Do I personally have to do this?"
If not, delegate the item.

★★★ 325 ★★★

View your work life as a puzzle with too
many pieces. Throw some out.

★★★ 326 ★★★

Well in advance of a meeting, notify
participants of the time, place and purpose.
Distribute copies of the agenda and indicate any
special participation required.

★★★ 327 ★★★

Use a central bulletin board to post one copy of an announcement rather than making, addressing, labeling and distributing individual copies.

★★★ 328 ★★★

To keep costs down, do not read, write or ponder online.

★ ★ ★ 329 ★ ★ ★

When trying to determine whether to
computerize or not to computerize a function,
ask this question: Is it faster for me to do
it manually? If the answer is yes, keep it manual.

171

★ ★ ★ 330 ★ ★ ★

Whenever you touch a piece of paper, move it
one step closer to completion.

* * * 331 * * *

If you make an appointment well in advance,
call the day before to confirm that the
meeting is still on.

* * * 332 * * *

Where appropriate, automate calendars,
to-do lists, name and address directories, and
planning information by using a computerized
personal information management system.

★ ★ ★ 333 ★ ★ ★

Work at a relaxed and reasonable pace.
Take breaks. Learn to relax.

★ ★ ★ 334 ★ ★ ★

Always tell the truth, but learn to do so in a way
that does not offend.

★★★ 335 ★★★

Work elimination should accompany job
elimination. Streamline the processes and
procedures to support the smaller
number of people.

174

★★★ 336 ★★★

Write in a way that comes naturally.
To avoid sounding stilted, have a conversation
with your reader.

★ ★ ★ 337 ★ ★ ★

If you travel, eat breakfast in your room.
Put on your suit last to avoid the risk of
wrinkles and stains.

★ ★ ★ 338 ★ ★ ★

175

Don't trust what the manufacturer says.
If it's important, bring another battery for your
wireless microphone or bulb for your
overhead projector.

★ ★ ★ 339 ★ ★ ★

Your first obligation is to look out for yourself,
your interests and your priorities. No one
will do this for you.

★ ★ ★ 340 ★ ★ ★

Don't undervalue your own time, energy
and resources.

★★★ 341 ★★★

Before moving your office to a new location,
hire a professional to help with the planning,
search and packing phases.

★★★ 342 ★★★

177

If you routinely work 60-, 70- or 80-hour weeks,
slowly start cutting back your workweek.
Leave 30 minutes earlier each day for a month
until you return to a normal 40-hour workweek.

★★★ 343 ★★★

Strive for excellence,
not perfection. Very few things
warrant the time and energy to
make them perfect.

178

★ ★ ★ 344 ★ ★ ★

Always start your meetings on time, even if
some of the participants are late.
You will develop a reputation for promptness.

★ ★ ★ 345 ★ ★ ★

Always end a meeting on time. Allot an
appropriate amount of time for each item on the
agenda commensurate with its worth.

★★★ 346 ★★★

Your electronic files and paper files should
carry the same headings.

★★★ 347 ★★★

When working on multiple projects,
keep each in a different-colored folder.

⋆ ⋆ ⋆ 348 ⋆ ⋆ ⋆

Write the phone number next to the person's name in your appointment book. You have a handy contact number to confirm or let him or her know of any change in plans.

181

⋆ ⋆ ⋆ 349 ⋆ ⋆ ⋆

If you have a choice of several hotels of equal quality, conduct your business at the one nearest the airport.

★ ★ ★ 350 ★ ★ ★

Actively reduce the number of reports you generate. Work with your supervisor and staff to identify reports that may be repetitive or that can be shortened. Cull your distribution list regularly.

182

★ ★ ★ 351 ★ ★ ★

Get off mailing and routing lists that serve no purpose and drop subscriptions to periodicals that repeat information provided elsewhere.

★ ★ ★ 352 ★ ★ ★

Learn the fine art of ignoring problems that
will solve themselves or will never need to be
solved. Consider the rule of three:
Wait three days on any significant issue.
In that period, it has resolved itself or intensified
and proved worthy of your attention.

183

★ ★ ★ 353 ★ ★ ★

Embrace change. It's going to happen whether
you like it or not.

★ ★ ★ 354 ★ ★ ★

Don't underestimate the amount
of time it will take you to get
all your papers and files
computerized.

184

★ ★ ★ 355 ★ ★ ★

Turn down new clients when you know you should. Every time.

★ ★ ★ 356 ★ ★ ★

Beware of false savings. Three hours of your assembly or installation time is not free.

★ ★ ★ 357 ★ ★ ★

Highlight key items the first time you
read a document.

★ ★ ★ 358 ★ ★ ★

To reduce the number of catalogs sent to your
business, write to Direct Marketing Association,
Mail Preference Service, P.O. Box 9008,
Farmingdale, NY 11735-9008. Request that your
name be removed from the list.

186

★ ★ ★ 359 ★ ★ ★

Prior to dictating, outline what you have to say.
While dictating, state all punctuation
where it occurs.

★ ★ ★ 360 ★ ★ ★

187

When mailing something important or using
bulk mail, include yourself in the mailing.
This way you can identify when the post office
actually delivered it in your city.

★ ★ ★ 361 ★ ★ ★

Keep in mind that there is no decision
that is risk-free. Good decisions simply
minimize the risk.

★ ★ ★ 362 ★ ★ ★

Leasing is often easier and more
cost-effective than ownership.
Thoroughly investigate your options.

188

★ ★ ★ 363 ★ ★ ★

Don't reinvent the wheel. Someone else
has faced a similar situation. If it is not
proprietary, borrow the idea, technique or
method and adapt liberally.

189

★ ★ ★ 364 ★ ★ ★

Use only one in-box for new information.
Having more than one can be a
procrastination trap.

⋆ ⋆ ⋆ 365 ⋆ ⋆ ⋆

Continually assess your quality of
work and your effectiveness.
Watch for creeping bad habits,
outdated processes and
poor organization.

INDEX

191

Index entries are by page.

ODETTE POLLAR is a nationally recognized author, trainer, speaker and organizing expert who directs the Oakland, California, firm Time Management Systems. Pollar travels nationally consulting and delivering programs that enhance performance, improve office management and streamline day-to-day operations.

Pollar is the author of two previous books: *Organizing Your Workspace: A Guide to Personal Productivity* (Crisp Publications, 1992) and *Dynamics of Diversity: Strategic Programs for Your Organization* (Crisp Publications, 1994). She writes a regular business column for two national magazines, *Contemporary Times* and *Successful Meetings*.

Pollar has worked in public and private agencies, corporations and professional associations. She founded Time Management Systems in 1979 and uses her 15 years' experience as a management consultant, writer and entrepreneur in her work with clients. A recognized expert on time management and organizational issues, she frequently appears in the media.

In her consulting work, Pollar shows professionals easy, effective ways to manage time, track projects and activities, create a workable filing system, simplify paperwork and streamline work flow. Her corporate clients include Levi Strauss, McDonald's, Hewlett Packard, Shell Oil, VISA and Pacific Bell.

Here is how to communicate with Pollar. Write Time Management Systems, 1441 Franklin Street, Suite 301, Oakland, CA 94612.

196

> I am interested in (check all that apply):
>
> ❑ Keynote speeches
> ❑ Training and seminars
> ❑ Personal improvement products
> ❑ An individual consultation
>
> Please attach your business card.

A Personal Note from the Author

I want to hear from you. Please write me with your feelings about this book, as well as any suggestions or comments. I am particularly interested in the results you receive from using the ideas in this book.

Upcoming editions in the *365 Ways* series will cover additional business simplification tips and ideas for simplifying your personal life. I welcome your response.

Here is what I think. . . .

1. This is what I liked and found helpful about the book: _____

_____

2. These are the specific tips I used and the results:

_____

_____

3. Suggestions for improvement: _____

_____

_____

198

Want to Share a Tip?

The idea(s) I have used to simplify my work life:

_____

_____

_____

I give you permission to use the above information in
your next book, *365 More Ways to Simplify Your Work Life.*

Name: _____

Address: _____

Signature: _____

Date: _____ Phone: _____

Thank You